better together*

*This book is best read together, grownup and kid.

 akidsco.com

a kids book about

a kids book about

Israel & Palestine

by Reza Aslan

a kids book about

Text copyright © 2024 by Reza Azlan.
Design copyright © 2024 by A Kids Book About, Inc.

Copyright is good! It ensures that work like this can exist, and more work in the future can be created.

All rights reserved. No part of this publication may be reproduced, distributed, or transmitted in any form or by any means, including photocopying, recording, other electronic or mechanical methods, without the prior written permission of the publisher, except in the case of brief quotations embodied in critical reviews and certain other noncommercial uses permitted by copyright law. For permission requests, write to the publisher.

A Kids Book About, Kids Are Ready, and the colophon 'a' are trademarks of A Kids Book About, Inc.

Printed in the United States of America.

A Kids Book About books are available online: *akidsco.com*

To share your stories, ask questions, or inquire about bulk purchases (schools, libraries, and nonprofits), please use the following email address: *hello@akidsco.com*

Print ISBN: 979-8-89281-016-6
Ebook ISBN: 979-8-89281-017-3

Designed and edited by Jelani Memory

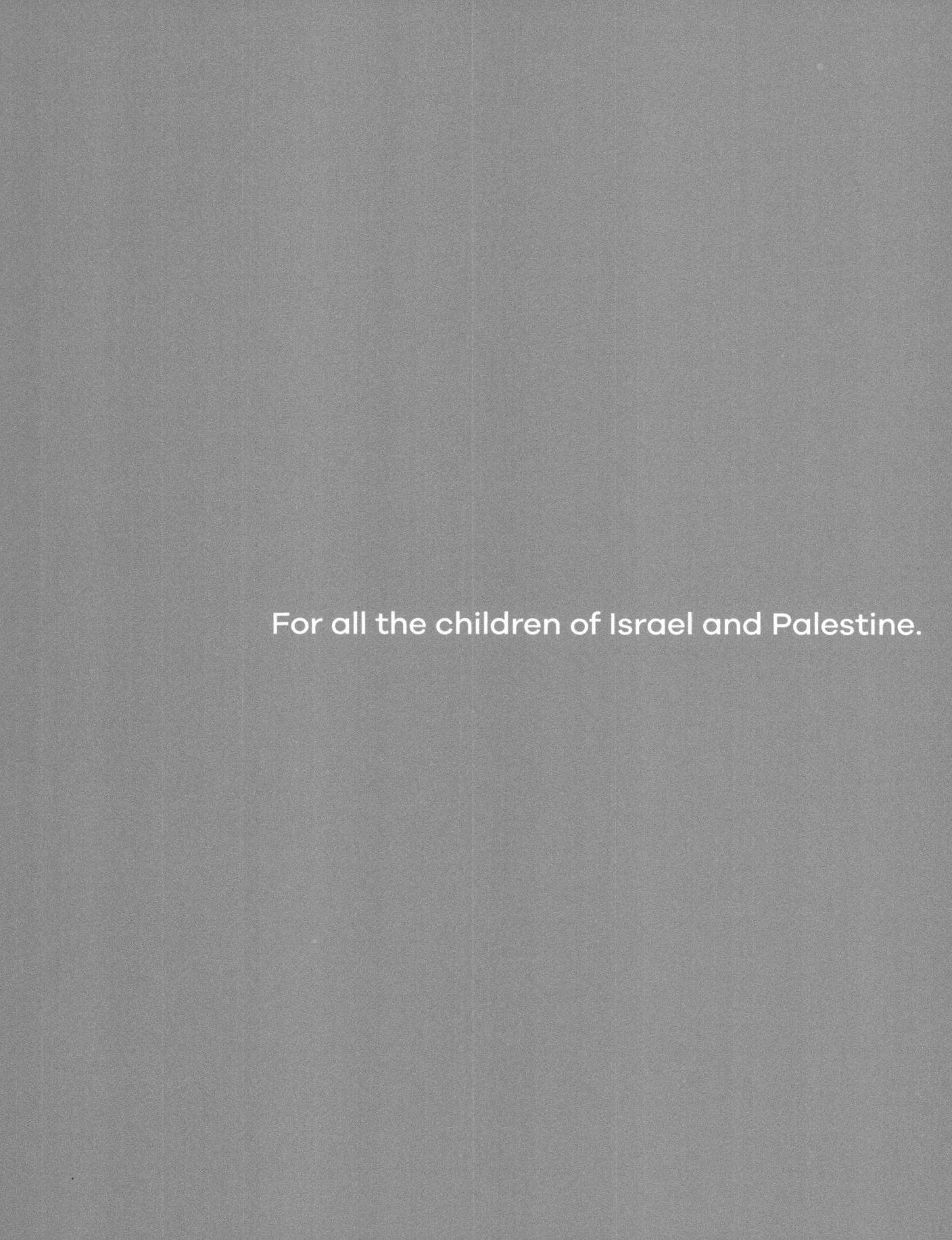

For all the children of Israel and Palestine.

Intro

Explaining the Israeli-Palestinian conflict to kids with fairness and simplicity is no easy task. Most grownups have trouble talking to each other about it!

This book is designed to give kids an overview of both sides of this conflict, without casting blame or painting either side as right or wrong. It is written specifically to help counter the stereotypes and prejudices that so often arise from a lack of factual information.

Although there are no easy answers when it comes to Israel and Palestine, simply learning about the key experiences, perspectives, and challenges of the people involved in this long-standing conflict can help cultivate empathy in children. It can teach kids to see the world through others' eyes, promoting compassion and a sense of shared humanity.

My hope is that children will learn that differences can coexist peacefully, and thus lay the groundwork for a more hopeful and inclusive future.

Hello.

My name is Reza and I've spent most of my life writing and talking about religion and politics, 2 things people take VERY seriously...

Religion helps people think about big ideas like God and the meaning of life.

Politics helps people come up with rules for how we can all live together as a society.

And when it comes to the subject of this book—
the conflict between Israel and Palestine—
you may have been hearing A LOT of talk recently.

That's understandable.
This teeny-tiny part of the
world gets **a ton** of attention.

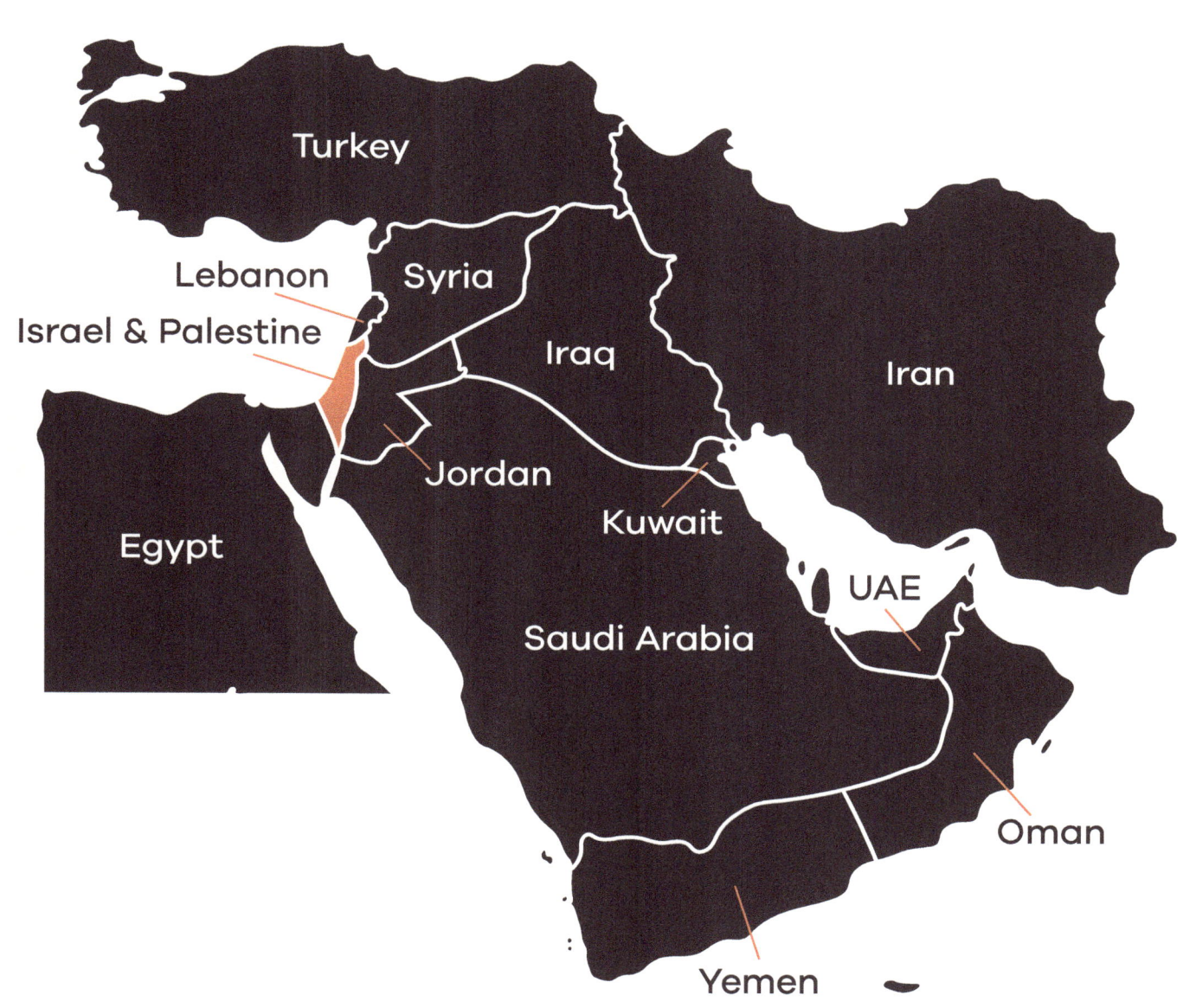

After all, we're talking about a place that is **special** to **Jews**, **Muslims**, and **Christians**, who together make up almost half of the world's population.

No wonder so many people refer to this place as the **Holy Land.**

If that weren't enough, many powerful countries around the world have used the conflict between Israel and Palestine for their own purposes.

Often, that means they make decisions which may be good for their own countries, but aren't so good for Israelis or Palestinians.

You can see why this
is such a complicated issue,
which can sometimes make
it hard to talk about.

But I bet you know as well as I do that you're never going to solve a problem unless you can talk calmly about it. And the only way to do that is to be willing to listen to the other side.

So then, let's tell this complicated story from both sides... the best that we can.

Over time, this small part of the world has had many names: Canaan, Israel, Judea, the Southern Levant, and Syria-Palaestina are just a few.

But, for much of the last thousand years or so, it has primarily been known as Palestine.

Whatever people have called this place, **Jews**, **Muslims**, **Christians**, and a whole bunch of other religious groups have been sharing this land for a very, very, very long time—going about their daily lives, practicing their religion, and more or less getting along with each other.

Then, about 100 years ago, the world was rocked first by one, and then by a second,

ld war.

Tens of millions of people were killed, and many millions more were displaced.*

*To be displaced means to be forced to leave your home or land.

During the Second World War,
something truly horrible happened.

All across Europe, millions of Jewish people were forced from their homes, taken to concentration camps, and killed by people who hated them simply because they were Jewish.

This terrible period is known as the Holocaust, and when it was over, nearly **half** of all the Jewish people in the world were dead.

Many Jewish people trying to escape the terrors of the Holocaust fled Europe to other parts of the world. Some went to the land they regarded as the Jewish historical home, in Palestine.

Pales

At the time, Palestine was one of many predominantly Arab lands in the Middle East that were controlled by Great Britain.

Britain supported Jewish immigration*
to Palestine and was even open to
the idea of establishing within it a
separate national home for
the **Jewish people**.

*Immigration means to leave your home
and travel to another country to live there.

But many people who had been living in Palestine for generations were against the idea of dividing the land into 2 separate states.

They wanted **a single independent Palestinian state**, no longer under British control.

This sparked a lot of conflict about the

land,

and how to fairly **share** it,
so everyone living there
could feel **safe** and **valued**.*

*To be valued means to be loved and respected for who you are.

When the Second World War ended, Britain's leaders turned to the newly formed United Nations for help finding a solution that would work for everyone.

UN

The United Nations, or UN, is an international organization made up of countries from around the globe who work together to try to solve the world's problems.

1947

In 1947, the UN came to the decision to split the land of Palestine into 2 different countries—

one which would be a national home for Jewish people called **Israel**, and the other an independent Arab nation called **Palestine**.

For many Jewish people who wanted to create a country of their own, this was an **acceptable** solution.

But for most everyone else in Palestine, this solution was **unacceptable** for a lot of reasons, one of which was that the Arabs were given less than 1/2 of the land, even though they made up 2/3 of the population.

By 1948, the United Nations still couldn't get everyone to agree to its proposal.

So, on May 14, 1948,
Israel declared itself a state.

948

The very next day, a group of Arab countries declared war on the new nation of Israel on behalf of the Palestinian people.

Although it was much smaller and greatly outnumbered, **Israel ultimately won the war**.

In fact, by the time the fighting was over, Israel had gained **much** more land than the UN had originally assigned to it.

During the war hundreds of Palestinian villages were destroyed, thousands of Palestinians were killed, and nearly a million Palestinians were forced out of their homes. Many fled to neighboring countries where, to this day, they and their children are still living as refugees.*

*A refugee is someone who has been forced to flee their home because of persecution, war, or violence.

Palestinians refer to this terrible event as the Nakba, which means "the catastrophe."

They had become a people
without a country of their own.

akba

Over the next few decades, Israel and its neighboring Arab countries fought many more wars against each other.

And Israel continued to win those wars, each time gaining more and more Palestinian territory.

50s   60s   70s   80s

Today, Israel is mostly at peace with its neighbors. It's been a long time since war has broken out between them.

| 90s | 00s | 10s | 20s |

At the same time, Israel continues to expand its territory further into the land which was supposed to be Palestine.

It has done this through what are called settlements.

Settlements are places where only Israelis are allowed to live—some are the size of cities.

The United Nations considers Israel's settlements to be illegal, not just because they are built on Palestinian land, but also because building them can mean destroying Palestinian homes in order to make room for Israeli ones.

And so, while Israel kept getting bigger and bigger, what was supposed to be Palestine kept getting smaller and smaller, and no one seemed to be doing anything about it.

Some Palestinians

began to resist the presence of Israeli settlements on their land. They held protests and marches to get the world to pay attention to what was happening to them.

But a small minority of Palestinians felt that wasn't enough…they began attacking and killing innocent Israeli people.

Israel responded to these attacks on their citizens with overwhelming military force. But this created more anger and violence from Palestinians, which then created an even more forceful response from Israel, and so on, and so on, and so on.

This is called a cycle of violence, and once it starts, it's **very** hard to stop.

But stopping the cycle of violence is exactly what nearly every Palestinian and Israeli wants to do.

And so, in the 1990s, with the world's support, the 2 sides sat down together to discuss how to fairly share the land they both love so much.

It has been many years since those conversations first began, but unfortunately, we are no closer to an independent Israel and an independent Palestine living side by side in peace.

That's because there are people on both sides who have no intention of sharing the land.

And they are doing whatever they can to make sure there will never be a peaceful solution to the conflict.

—————————————— **And so we're stuck.**

Sometimes when you're stuck, it helps to look at the problem from the other person's point of view.

When you read the history of this conflict, it's clear there have been times when both sides have done a LOT of things wrong.

They've each caused the other pain and suffering.

They both have reason to feel angry and afraid.

But the only way we'll ever be able to bridge the divide between Israel and Palestine is to try to understand both views of the story.

What does that mean?

It means acknowledging and healing from the problems of the past.

Most of all, it means recognizing that both sides want the same thing: to feel safe, secure, and valued in a country they can call their own.

Being able to see both sides of a conflict can be a kind of superpower.

It means you have what it takes to be a

peacemaker.

And if we are ever going to solve this conflict with fairness and justice, it is going to take people like you who recognize…

There is more that
connects the people of

Israel and

Palestine

than there is driving them apart.

Discussion Time!

Let's ask ourselves some questions about what we've just read.

1. Why do you think it's important to listen to both sides of a story, even if you don't agree with one side?

2. How do you think we can help people in Israel and Palestine feel safe, secure, and valued?

3. What does it mean to be a peacemaker? Can you think of ways you can be a peacemaker in your own life?

4. Can you think of a time when you tried to see things from someone else's point of view? How did it make you feel?

5. What does the word "conflict" mean? Can you think of a time when you had a disagreement with someone? How did you solve it?

6. Why do you think people take religion and politics so seriously?

7. What is a "cycle of violence"? Can you think of ways to stop it?

8. What does it mean to be a refugee? Can you imagine what it might feel like to be forced to leave your home and go to a new place?

9. Why do you think the people of Palestine and Israel couldn't agree on how to share the land in 1947 and 1948? What would help them today?

10. If you represented a country which was a member of the United Nations, how would you work to resolve the conflict in Israel and Palestine?

11. What do you think we can do to promote peace and understanding in the world, even when conflicts seem very complicated?

Outro

Having read this brief history of Israel and Palestine, hopefully you've recognized that there is no simple solution to this conflict. But that's OK! Sometimes just asking the right questions is enough.

Create a safe space for children to express their thoughts and explore their uncertainties. Discuss how people can work together to make things better and emphasize the importance of finding peaceful solutions and compromise. People can have different perspectives without ignoring their common humanity.

Encourage the kids in your life to walk in the shoes of individuals on both sides. Know that simply by nurturing empathy, you can cultivate a garden where understanding blooms and the roots of tolerance deepen.

About The Author

Reza Aslan (he/him) always wanted to be a writer. But his mom told him he had to get a "real job" first. So, he spent years at school earning a bunch of degrees so he could become a scholar of religions.

Now, he gets to do both of those things: study religion and write books!

A recipient of the prestigious James Joyce Award, Reza has written several internationally bestselling books, including the #1 New York Times Bestseller, *Zealot: The Life and Times of Jesus of Nazareth*.

Reza is also an Emmy- and Peabody-nominated scholar and public intellectual who tries to help people make sense of the sometimes nonsensical things we all do in the name of religion and politics.

 rezaaslan.com

Discover more at akidsco.com

Printed in the USA
CPSIA information can be obtained
at www.ICGtesting.com
CBHW041259220324
5712CB00012B/443